FOUNDATIONS OF OUR NATION

CREATING THE
CONSTITUTION

by Wil Mara

FOCUS READERS

WWW.FOCUSREADERS.COM

Focus Readers is distributed by North Star Editions:
sales@northstareditions.com | 888-417-0195

Produced for Focus Readers by Red Line Editorial.

Content Consultant: Dr. Gideon Mailer, Associate Professor of History, University of Minnesota Duluth

Photographs ©: Billion Photos/Shutterstock Images, cover, 1, North Wind Picture Archives, 4–5, 7, 9, 10–11, 15, 19 (bottom), 23, 27, 29, Everett Historical/Shutterstock Images, 12, 16–17, 19 (top), 19 (middle), Art Collection 3/Alamy, 21, Everett - Art/Shutterstock Images, 24–25

ISBN
978-1-63517-243-0 (hardcover)
978-1-63517-308-6 (paperback)
978-1-63517-438-0 (ebook pdf)
978-1-63517-373-4 (hosted ebook)

Library of Congress Control Number: 2017935930

Printed in the United States of America
Mankato, MN
June, 2017

ABOUT THE AUTHOR

Wil Mara is the author of more than 200 books, many of which are educational titles for children. His interest in American history goes back to his childhood, spurred in part by a trip to Washington, DC, in the late 1970s during which he met President Jimmy Carter.

TABLE OF CONTENTS

CHAPTER 1

ARTICLES OF CONFEDERATION

In 1776, American colonists declared their **independence** from Great Britain. At this time, the two sides were already at war. The American Revolutionary War (1775–1783) had started because of disagreements about British control.

During the war, the Continental Congress served as the government.

The American Revolutionary War began in April 1775 at the Battles of Lexington and Concord.

This group was made up of **delegates** from each of the 13 states. They made important decisions for the new nation. For instance, they made **treaties** with other countries. They issued money. They made sure the army had enough soldiers and supplies.

Some states already had their own constitutions. These documents set the rules for how the state governments were organized. But members of the Congress wanted a government that had more control over all 13 states. This idea was known as a **federal** government.

The Congress chose 13 of its members to write a new constitution. They created

The Continental Congress put George Washington in charge of the American army.

a document known as the Articles of Confederation. Members of the Congress debated the document for months. For example, how much power should the states have? How much power should the federal government have over the states?

How should the federal government be structured? How should the government collect the money it needed?

The Congress took more than a year to write the Articles of Confederation. But in November 1777, the document was finally ready. The first article made it clear that the new nation would be called the United States of America.

The Congress sent the Articles to the 13 states for their approval. This process was known as **ratification**. The Articles would not be official until all 13 states ratified it. Meanwhile, the war for independence continued.

John Dickinson led the group that wrote the Articles of Confederation.

CHAPTER 2

PROBLEMS DEVELOP

Virginia ratified the Articles of Confederation in December 1777. The other states took longer. Many of them wanted more changes. However, the Congress refused to consider these changes. Finally, the last state ratified the Articles in early 1781.

The war was nearly over by the time the last state ratified the Articles of Confederation.

The new federal government took effect in March 1781. It was known as the

ARTICLES OF CONFEDERATION

	State	Date Ratified
1	Virginia	December 16, 1777
2	South Carolina	February 5, 1778
3	New York	February 6, 1778
4	Rhode Island	February 9, 1778
5	Connecticut	February 12, 1778
6	Georgia	February 26, 1778
7	New Hampshire	March 4, 1778
8	Pennsylvania	March 5, 1778
9	Massachusetts	March 10, 1778
10	North Carolina	April 5, 1778
11	New Jersey	November 19, 1778
12	Delaware	February 1, 1779
13	Maryland	February 2, 1781

Congress of the Confederation. Then, in September of that year, British soldiers surrendered. The United States had won the war.

However, the Congress of the Confederation did not last long. Its members quickly realized the Articles had several flaws. The main problem was that the new federal government was weak. Most of the power remained with the state governments. And this caused many problems.

For example, the federal government needed money. It had a lot of **debt** to foreign countries. After all, the war for independence had been very expensive.

The federal government also needed money to run its operations. To bring in money, the government created taxes. But the Articles did not say the states had to pay these taxes. For this reason, many states didn't pay.

Also, the federal government did not have a national army. Instead, the government relied on the states' **militias**. Many leaders disliked this system. They feared it would be difficult to gather a military force if the nation had to protect itself.

In September 1786, delegates from several states called for a meeting. They wanted to improve the Articles of

George Washington led the Constitutional Convention.

Confederation. Their meeting began in May 1787. It became known as the Constitutional Convention.

The delegates soon realized that fixing the Articles was not enough. The country needed a whole new form of government.

CHAPTER 3

THE VIRGINIA PLAN

The delegates discussed many options for a new government. One idea was known as the Virginia Plan. This plan got its name because James Madison, the delegate who created it, was from Virginia. Madison's plan called for a government with three branches.

James Madison later became the president of the United States.

The three branches would create a system of checks and balances. Each branch would have some power over the others. That way, one branch would not have too much power.

The first branch would make laws. It was known as the legislative branch. This branch would have two parts. One was the Senate, and the other was the House of Representatives. Together, they were known as Congress.

The second branch would **enforce** the laws that Congress created. It was known as the executive branch. The head of this branch would be the country's president. The president would be in charge of the military. The president could also create groups to make sure people followed the law.

The third branch would decide if laws did not follow the Constitution.

CREATING THE VIRGINIA PLAN

James Madison had help from other delegates when he created the Virginia Plan.

George Mason was in favor of the rights of people and of the states. He wanted to make sure the new government had a limit to its powers.

Charles Pinckney argued for a strong federal government. He was also in favor of slavery.

Roger Sherman wanted to make sure every state was represented fairly. He supported the idea of a legislative branch with two houses.

It was known as the judicial branch. The judicial branch was made up of courts and judges. There would be different levels of courts. Each would hear different types of legal cases. Higher courts would have power over lower courts. The most powerful court in the country would be the Supreme Court.

The Constitutional Convention lasted nearly four months. Delegates had many debates. One major topic was how many people would **represent** each state in Congress. Smaller states wanted each state to have the same number of representatives. That way, every state would be equal. However, larger states

William Paterson of New Jersey wanted each state to have the same number of representatives.

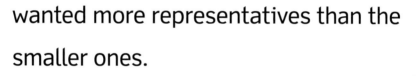

wanted more representatives than the smaller ones.

The solution was to have both. The Senate would be made up of two people from each state. But the House of Representatives would be different. States with large populations would have many representatives. States with small populations would have few.

DISAGREEMENT OVER SLAVERY

The topic of slavery caused one of the biggest debates at the meeting. George Mason was a delegate who held hundreds of slaves. However, he sometimes spoke out against slavery. "Every master of slaves is born a petty **tyrant**," he said. Luther Martin, another slaveholder, agreed with Mason. He said it was "dishonorable to the American character to have such a feature in the Constitution."

Enslaved black people worked on thousands of farms in the United States. Most of these farms were in southern states. White farm owners knew they would make less money without enslaved workers. Many delegates said they would not sign the Constitution if slavery was illegal. As a result, the Constitution allowed slavery to continue.

Enslaved people had to work under extremely difficult conditions.

Delegates also had to decide how to count enslaved people as part of the population. This would affect the number of representatives each state received. Southern states wanted enslaved people to count as part of the population. Northern states did not. In the end, delegates agreed on a compromise. Each slave would count as three-fifths of a person.

CHAPTER 4

RATIFICATION

The final draft of the Constitution was ready in September 1787. The document has seven sections in total. Each of these sections is known as an article. The first three articles describe the legislative, executive, and judicial branches.

George Washington was the first person to lead the executive branch.

Article Four explains all of the responsibilities that states have to one another. It also mentions the responsibilities between the states and the federal government. In addition, it describes how new states can join the country.

Article Five explains how the Constitution can be changed. Changes are known as amendments. Any amendment must be approved by three-fourths of the states.

Article Six states that the Constitution is the highest law in the country. That means all government workers have a duty to uphold the law.

People held a parade in New York City after the Constitution was ratified.

Article Seven explains ratification. The Constitution would become official when nine of the 13 states approved the document.

In December 1787, Delaware became the first state to ratify the Constitution.

27

Several more states approved the document that winter. In June 1788, the ninth state ratified the Constitution. The document was now official. It went into effect on March 4, 1789. This was the first day of the new US government.

The Constitution has gone through several changes over the years. The first 10 amendments are known as the Bill of Rights. They were ratified in 1791. These amendments describe the rights of all US citizens. These included freedom of religion, freedom of speech, and many other rights.

Today, there are 27 amendments to the Constitution. The government has made

People celebrated the Thirteenth Amendment in 1866.
This amendment made slavery illegal.

changes to keep up with the times. That
may be the reason for the document's
lasting success. The Constitution has
been in effect for more than 225 years.

FOCUS ON
THE CONSTITUTION

Write your answers on a separate piece of paper.

1. Write a letter to a friend explaining the main idea of Chapter 2.

2. Do you think larger states should have more representatives than smaller states? Why or why not?

3. When did the Constitutional Convention begin?

    A. July 1776
    B. September 1781
    C. May 1787

4. Why was it difficult for the government to collect taxes under the Articles of Confederation?

    A. because the government did not have a national military
    B. because the government did not have an executive branch
    C. because the government did not have enough representatives

Answer key on page 32.

GLOSSARY

debt
Money that must be paid back to another person or group.

delegates
People who speak on behalf of a larger group.

enforce
To make sure people follow a rule.

federal
Having to do with the top level of government.

independence
The ability to make decisions without being controlled by another government.

militias
Groups of citizens trained to carry out military actions, usually during times of emergency.

ratification
The act of giving something official approval.

represent
To speak on behalf of a larger group.

treaties
Agreements between two or more countries.

tyrant
A ruler who uses his or her power in a cruel way.

TO LEARN MORE

BOOKS

Lusted, Marcia Amidon. *The US Constitution*. Mankato, MN: The Child's World, 2016.

Schmidt, Maegan. *The US Constitution and Bill of Rights*. Minneapolis: Abdo Publishing, 2013.

Sonneborn, Liz. *The United States Constitution*. Chicago: Heinemann Library, 2013.

NOTE TO EDUCATORS

Visit **www.focusreaders.com** to find lesson plans, activities, links, and other resources related to this title.

INDEX